3.7 SHADES OF GRIEF

Vijay Ashok Indushokai

TANEESHA PUBLISHERS

Title : 3.7 Shades of Grief
Author : Vijay Ashok Indushokai
Edition : First (June, 2025)
ISBN : 9789349789548

Published by

TANEESHA PUBLISHERS | *A Venture by -* **PRACHI DIGITAL PUBLICATION**

Regd. Add.: 254, Khuriyakhatta No. 10, Bindukhatta,
Lalkuan, Nainital - 262402, Uttarakhand, India
Website : www.taneeshapublishers.in
E-mail : taneeshapublishers@gmail.com
Phone : +91 8454 812712, +91 8057 812712

Printed by :
Manipal Technologies Limited, Bengaluru - 560001, Karnataka

"In a time of deceit,
telling the truth is a revolutionary act."

- George Orwell

To

TATHAGAT BUDHHA

Index

My colossal nothingness

I see various colors in darkness and water and vice versa.
My colossal nothingness floats light within me
maybe to alight the enlighten loneliness with solitude lights

The comprehensive conclusions kill essence of being
Now I come to know that there is no meaning to love something
Words always play me although my fever is fewer
I have to be more conscious about consciousness

I seldom meet to myself in poetry

The shivering anecdotal lumps in the swollen existence
never allow me to be the me as I have been dreamt for.

I want to be an unconscious to be myself
an authentic genuine and merge it with consciousness
I don't want to switch my being with this worldly world.

It's not trustworthy
I seldom meet myself in poetry
and nowadays poetry itself is missing

The fragrance of naked souls can be found even in poetry
only the language shouldn't be deliberately civilized
Unnecessary breath can also be the hurdle for smooth life
that's why I hate flowers sometimes
The falsity is a real reality of entities
without changing the false; it's still false with its very essence.

Why should I believe in language as well?

I wish that if I were the most attached person for life in life
then I would have enjoyed the very essence of detachment
with its various hues with the bloody time.

The languages could have nurtured nature
but the hybridity of the essence
doesn't make any sense even with the sun.

Now nonsenses also don't have any nonsensical sense
to exist even as a commodity of language as well.
The feel in the very filled feelings
also don't have any solid entity
of its very abstractness as a being.

Even I am not feeling that emptiness
with alienation where I used to sip the loneliness
with very attached feelings of nothing.

Now I am being transformed
into an attached stranger
with myself without nothingness as well.
Why should I believe in language as well?

Blobs

I lost in nothing to find existence
I got solitude with utmost liveliness
it's alone with glad loneliness
that liquify fragrance of being

The very blobs of life also evaporate
with immortal thirst of ocean
that clouds shout for

Now there's no meaning to the wet of sweat
in your sweet world
where words and their meanings are in scrap
with their authentic genuineness

The erotic moralities are more porny
with betrayal faiths and loyalties
for the establishment of real human world
that's trying to accept the nudity
without and with utmost boast

I dangle on the very shore of poetry

The twoness is more one than the oneness itself
The semiconscious subconsciousness is nice conscious
with the concreteness of twilight of my essence

The semi-unconsciousness of my essence
is already lost in my existence itself in the deep unconscious
although I dangle on the very shore of poetry

Neve

I always lose myself in this lose life
which is already lost its loss in real reality
that I need to enjoy the loneliness omy being a mine own

My naive existence laves towards nothingness
to be neve being in this bloody world
and its naive realism of reality

I always lose myself in this lose life
which is already lost its loss in real reality
that I need to enjoy the loneliness of my being as mine own

My naive existence laves towards nothingness
to be neve being in this bloody world
and its naive realism of reality

Bogus

The rake of fake
personalities are utmost personnel's lake
For fishing a fish is used to hunt
so fish deceive fish even in a lake
The humans with humanity seem the same with advance fake

The bloody philosophy to seek meaning
in meaninglessness of life in worthless life is futility
I always condemn your boastful reality
and bogus life, its philosophy with its guaranteed utility
The life should be life and the world should be the world
with all free and required creativity

The used path of life is being set immortal
even a new invented ways and path are also set immortal

Self-convincer

I am trapped and caged for a while
but when I break the cage to fly
somebody has stolen the free and infinite sky

Now they nurture me well in to grow my wings to fly high
They themselves have removed all the traps and cages
and made everyone free
They do not cut the wings
They just have stolen the sky to lose the ability to fly
They want our next generation even biologically without wings
or inactive genes of flying ability

They just want to make our next generation think
that flying is an illness and taboo
and the wings are burden of happy life
They want our reality to make rumors and nightmares
They are making us to be self-convincer of slavery
without any other option of life without slavery

Rein

Deceive me and enforce me
to make my mind to leave the dark
Seduce me and realizing me
the actuality of of my own actual me

Just convince me to get up
show me the very mirrors in minds
which are fascinated to haunt the reality of truth to show
Oh mind!
be thc Buddha to persuade me within
to break fortified walls and ports
to open the prisoner mind

Let the aliveness of nothing do its work
for what it seems still invisible
which is wide clear for an open and neutral mind
but the eyes even of the mind were always rein

An eyeful eye

She is tall of a seashore
with a hussy water whore
The drop of a pearly sweat
drop and drop in a sea never met

The donkeys are wise in the fools
The world runs smooth with philosophy of mules
The capability of even seashore is not farce
Which thing is in abundance and which one should be scarce?

The swollen humanity of swallowed world must be great
Poets and artists should be hanged and sensibles should be in threat
An eye for an eye is now an eyeful sight
The world is advanced and its future is bright

The last kiss

The last kiss that never reaches the lips
It initiated to freeze but is blowing with intensity rather
The memories of former warmth fatherly father
who also safely collect the tears and affinity keeps

The innocent scare of his entire being harness
with his tender childhood and hopes ruin
but still his glowing being catches father's fondness
his assumpted cruel mother snatches him
tearing father's affinity to ruin

Connotations, prejudices and assumptions of mother
never apply to everyone who give birth
The real nurturer can be strongly the father
although the majority for mother is true by birth

The forehead, the chin, the cheeks are eagerly waiting
and anguish for father's incomplete colossal kiss
which is still alive on father's lips
to give it his two years lad waiting
but this last kiss would be incomplete
and immortal on father's lips

Four and half years daughter's anguishes for
heavenly hug to father
to explore the meaning of life but
the mother smashes it even her eye

Every moment the daughter misses it
beyond the alphabetic security love of her father
and overfond attachment with utmost affinity that her mother can sly

An infinite question mark

Hypothetical truth cannot be proved
the ultimate truth anymore and vice versa,
although the quantum possibilities
cannot be denied for anything,
nothing and everything as well

Now it seems clear that the circumstances and consequences
are powerful with time and none of the motions and powers
(where it works and it's totally up to the creatures to think
who thinks that they think but it still depends on the former
and so on that can be go on)
I think thinking must be boring to the ones
who think they are the only powerful with great thinking

Who thinks what and what not
Who gets what and who caught what
Obtaining hypothesis is what
and what hypothetically not
An infinite question mark…

Gleam

The affinity-hurts bloom with glee of gloom
Mine being never negotiate with existential zoom

The extract of essence patiently becomes relish
I, the mindful caught myself destroying to perish

Your hellish gleam of life is suffused over
I condemn everything that you imposed me to accept ever

The hush of lush you proclaim morality
The bloody cultural hegemony is with immortality

The cruel innocence pretends the humanity
The origin of black-hole isn't in its singularity

The leaf that knows

The procrastinating being knows not
the essence of mine that the goal got

I, the predominant mind although haunted in this bloody world
and never allow even the sun to scorch and the snow to cold

The very nature that blooms my mind with zeal
the unconscientious can be felt awaken to kill

The leaf that knows everything about me
I am been again betrayed by weather also in glee

I showed pity and forgave even the ones who weren't prominent
It's a blunder of mine because they are making me everytime blunt

Who knows the breaths of octopus and of mine

Hegemonic glee that porked the mind
Glorious charm that angry on the grind

The hallucination of life is the life itself
Words manipulate minds with all bookshelf

Number four found guilty for holistic harmony
Playing the death with lovely all gloomy

Who knows the breaths of octopus and of mine
Changing worldly gender with all hearts nine

The sparkling murmur blows in water
The nature is dumb with sky's chatter

Poets found dead in cells of nothing
Protection should be invisible with transparent clothing

The abhangs ask

Anybody who doesn't waste time,
finds ample time even for the time
that he requires to spend
They postpone everything
even the polarities and moralities
wasted vest
I know the unknown things
that nap with polymer hacks and
trifle snacks
thirsty taste
Told stories are utmost untold
I read the unread hues that mold
the colors which paints transparency of concrete blows

The abhangs ask me to destroy the mending walls
and free the poetry from its slavery- freedom as well

Upcoming birds

The thicket disrespect of time
smoothly runs with picket hymn

The highest chirp of upcoming birds
with sky's loosened strings of life's chords

The ancient hues of white color knows
the peaceful anarchy and chaos' claws

The hoax never claims to be a being
though the world comes into its being

The knows never known the authentic reality
while the mysteries nail truth's wild ability

Your pious cultures excite

Pity's kindness also seems futile here with validity
Affection's affinity seems meme here with all its nudity

The scorching beings of here are nonsensical existence
The fibster grows with valor and its in persistence

The whisper of ears speaks serenity in tongue
cruelty oxyacetylene fosters the amazon of lung

The penned realities are compared with falsity
The porn of your pious cultures excite morality

The curious changing language and grammars all lie
The real value never comes true of authentic pie

The only zero truth is the truth of zero
The reasons lean high with notorious Nero

Teaching is not a thing that could be taught

Sometimes reality becomes hurdle to be awakened
The only truth is nothing
and whatever seems to be existed
as everything
has nothing
even the shadow of truth isn't there.

Teaching is not a thing that could be taught

All the Mahars in the world come together,
they buy an island and established their awakened,
intellectual and peaceful hightech Mahar country.

Your horizon flea

You give me the precious poison glee
My skies manipulate by your horizon flea

I canceled the race of cheetah with deary eyes
The speed was nice of cheat with the cruel free flies

It's a rape everywhere
even through eye and rye of sympathy named consent
Nature should select the natural selection
with evolutionary humans and their consent

Happiness is a curse

Happiness is a curse
I spread myself in cosmoverse

The cosmosapiens know my immortal grief
You can take a pile of time to know in brief

I created my mind and timely trap of time
If you want you can compose a bastard hymn

I anguish for humanity entire my life
now I have deleted the Earth and humans swipe

Contradict reality

A waterfall of authentic reality chooses
the ocean to be expressed through.
Now I came to know to whom I have to call a freedom-mule
Toppers are always toppers until
they don't (assume) make others inferior

Her confusion to be upset can be a season of the world.
She emits the eyely eyes through the eyes
the accepted and omniscient impositions of slavery are the living
inspirations now with their giant common consent of life.

Every hue of the shadow of being
can't be concealed by your awakened eyes
cruelty controls the quality as well
although
contradict reality yearns for justice
while justices justn't give justice
Everyone is chancy so one should be aware
that our genuine problem is others' best chance to exploit us

An immature dry of a wet sky

The languishing eyes should eyes for what
Answers are questioning what not and what
The catching expectations though seem nice and cute caught
The smile of ice ruins although it never be caught

An immature dry of a wet sky
I penetrate my being in a havoc's lie

A curious pie is a language of mine
It's a real darkness that always shine

The fear of fearlessness is now a secured life
A multi-dimensional pleasure is now scattered swipe

If you are expecting from a fool to make you wise

If you are expecting from a fool to make you wise
Then the life has meaning and meaninglessness nice
I don't want speak on assumptions and prejudice
I can understand the essence although I threw it thrice
I can endure the emotions, the creations from agonies
Its cruelty pretends oneness although is more than a lice

Why to play the string of humanity here knowing all
Everything is pretended pure and ethical
although is hybrid, bionic and splice

I can be nice every time but never compromise with self-respect
I cannot allow my mind anymore to be ruined and slice

My daughter sprouts sky even in soil

Whenever she utters a word
a melody always sings a bird

Flowers sip their utmost beauty
Fragrance honestly does its duty

I wish her morning freedom-day
Brooks are used to sprinkle hey

My daughter sprouts sky even in soil
Before her ownness an ocean could coil

A father can be immortal in daughter's zeal
An affection can be mortal but it always feel

How a father can talk before his girl's view
She is giving life's philosophical preview

'I' is nothing although nothing is true.
The falsity's shadow shows ultimate true

The death of poet knows mine is dead
No one assures, whether the mind is in head.

Wilfred Owen and the spontaneous imposed patriotism

A suppressed perennial river
and mine overload mind
cannot commit suicide anymore

A floating fragrant flower
never smell itself utensils death
A shivering dawn never bet with dusk
comparing me with the skyish boredom
A messy peace of mind
and the very brooks in my mind
are unable to be enable as nature

I can balance between my existence and essence
if emptiness of solitude alone allows me
to be the one as a whole.

I crumple my heart to ash
I really don't want to live here
I want to be an existence-smash
I want the bloody supernova to clear

The witty wit of the wits with torn paper
never tore the tear of mine

The hikes and its pipe
are always balanced the nature
Although
The mess has serenity with maze insanity
that breaks the unbreakable laws of nation
Wilfred Owen and the spontaneous imposed patriotism
should be analyzed unbiasedly

Poetryness

The abrupt and emerging hues of adolescence
are still emerging as fragrance to crumble in culture
and so called civilization

The only way to live
is to be exploited here
removing the originality

The signs of buds
are not yet that much mature
to be matured as a flower

I can consider the nature natural
if I assume bias assumptions of your world

I can manage broken Abhangas
with poetry but the poetryness should be poetic
no matter
whether it's with the poetic justice or not

How does a calf withdraw the silk-milk of its own mother?

The measured smile of Monalisa
maybe a pleasure for my pleasure principle
but my artistic eyes couldn't find
golden ratio in pretended humanity

Brought respect of the flower of Neem
can be converted into spherical being
in these humanistic realms
where beings are also found
being-less with all respects

When the humans stop pretending humanity
which is more pompous than the boastfulness

How does a calf withdraw the silk-milk of its own mother?

No utterance

I myself is a contradict

No utterance

I myself is an utterance

No sense

I myself a sensible none

No beliefs

The beliefs determine myself

The betrayal

The deception ruins the I

The mind is stuck in my net

Humus expectations dry the wet
The mind is stuck in my net

She languished every moment for
And wants to live the moment more

The bud's wet and fragrant nod
Unconnected connection and its cod

The scared sacred nectar's wish
Deserted-ocean and lively fish

The assumpted navel and biased cord
The mind's birth and mental ward

She signed for nothing and more
Her smile is whole and eyes are core

There is no need of life to be lived

Your blunder offense is just that
you inspire us to be an atheist
giving logical and scientific awakening.
You should stop this nonsense at earliest ,
you are hazard to our ideal society
There is no need of life to be lived

Actually imagination is the originator of reality

Imagination is not imaginary at all,
imaginary truths and realities maybe
neither mindly activities nor mind itself imaginary
Actually imagination is the originator of reality
even abstract to concrete and vice versa

A whistle went through my heart

Fraction of desires blinking in her eyes
How long the distinguishment will be the authentic as truth

A cute clean hug of nothing smiles at me with gorgeous eyes
The playing innocence on the sand has been vanished

It came back with a materialistic hue.
The language without words is the actual language
otherwise there is no synonyms in any language of words
A whistle went through my heart.

You enforce me daily to sing life's bloody hymn

No one knows what's there in the mind of time
although it plays everyone, every moment with rhyme

I let me exploit for emotions and essence that's my crime
You enforce me daily to sing life's bloody hymn

How I ruin my heart it doesn't matter at all
The running as well as race itself made to fall

My liveliness, existence and the essence always call
although the nature never cover with worldly shadow and its mall

I the one who condemns everything still alive
The bees and their nature never manipulate their hive

Loneliness is my soul mate

The hating affection of loved nothing
emerges the true solitude in me to be myself
as loneliness is my soul mate

I can never distinguish between anything
nor in my existence and my mind

The possible possibilities can possibly determine me
but the real determination of exalted being
should be normalized as true human being

I can now find the exact difference between the wings of birds
and the flight even with golden ratio and life

Mirrors of existence mimic the imitation

A crystal of wave with its vibration is found in my mind
The very mirrors of existence mimic the imitation of nothing
to be stored in that trillion hexa-terabyte crystal

I peer within for me but the sought yet to be discovered

The lumps of love and compassion are false to lie
until the revelation of pity reveals

There is only one truth exists in your world that there is no lie
but the manipulation of truth and dimensional reality

The promising frequency of her being

Her blasting mind evaporates tender innocent being
with pubic dune dame
She spreads herself in the universe with nordic perfume

I can realize the dimensional vibrations of her within
Her subconscious signs to be fried as cumin

The society with its obligations hooks her kind
She has ability to ruin assumptions and traditions to grind

The promising frequency of her being emits
through her every particle and mind
The inner open eyed awakened through eyeless
but he never be blind

The hopelessness of mine not to connect with
although she deserves gleam
The universe ruins herself if a thirst not be fulfilled
with a fragrant slim

How do I be in this bloodiest world?

Why did I forget all the cruelties,
the agonies and traces of emotional ruin?
Hornets and ants can build the new utopia
with bees and their multi-universal skills but
How do I be in this bloodiest world?

I cannot believe in Shakespeare

I myself revolt within me to be myself
I rebel even to family which is more than myself

The very enforcement to be a selfish (being myself)
is from irritation to the peace
and even to the piece of heart for perhaps peace of mind

I cannot believe in Shakespeare
with his utmost literariness
because I don't know the reason of anything and everything
actually knowing it also doesn't matter for the truth

Truth is not mere beauty
even beauty is not a truth at all.
The smiling carcasses
can answer the questions of living livelihood

The mourning morning always smiles

The fatigue of pity and the dizzy of existence emerge
a non-aesthetic aestheticism in me to live

The very contradiction of nothing and the bloody similes of life
encourage me which always bores me to be human beings

The mourning morning always smiles
at me to husk the dusk
But the penalty of mind never knows the pusy grief
of the atlantic ocean hidden within it

I am ready to assume mind the disk of hypnotism
but the aesthetic beauty of utmost egoist beauty
beautify the fluid if flower's nectar for bees
with the sunny hues of the sky

I can weave my mind

The artificial happiness and smile of robot
can sprout the fertility of land to be more aesthetic
with wet emotions for catharsis of life

The extreme essence that lures for life
can languish for mortal immortality
but the pleasure and satisfaction always
lay on the same contradict thread
I can weave my mind with

Let me deceive myself to believe in

Let me deceive myself to believe in
Crumbling mind with being akin

I dismantle the ideology to be me
Why the eagle should stand on knee

The Phoenix renders within me always
My mind catches fireflies of mine all ways

The envy nature and Frued's cigar lights
The unconscious torches to the nights

The lucid dreams and icebergs hallucinates nature
I have to hunt the darkness to be a catcher

The butcher's pity maybe more than empathy
The utmost pitious kindness maybe apathy

Acedia

A living hell in the said heaven
always mislead the honest deed
of fascinated fool; a theist

A blind flames never light the lights
which are unenlightened from ever
it lighted up even as sacred lamps

The contradiction between
the mugging up hymns and
the reality of them is really contradict
without any figure of speech

The end of the meanings in languages
and their syntax never determine anything
and influence everything is a curse
to the fragrance of the nature
and the golden ratio; an artificial naturality

The bionic DNA and robotic affection
now no longer seem artificial
although intelligence is a creativity of acedia.

Thrice-versa

Your assumptions of freedom and liberty
actually you believe are illness
if appears in its authentic and original forms

your tore skies never been stitched;
you blow with your darkened lights
I even tear all layers of my existence through my mind.

I can awake the unconsciousness to paint the reality
of subconscious, conscious and thrice -versa
I can see Murakami on Kafka's shore
though I am not sure about mine.

Coping

I shouldn't be merciful even on myself as well
The scorchingness of humanity is unable
to be the most boastful as it's practiced for centuries

I can wet the oceans for their own thirsts
but the crust of harmony yet to be break

The right time to hang hopes has come
although you are hoping with all the hops for hopes

The slopes are opened up now with pleasurable gratification
I anguish for nothingness where nothing remains nothing

The languished beauties poke me with coping
at the edge of infinite universe and its very cop with my mind

Poignant verve

Poignant verve meekly strikes me
to live the rudimentary bloody life of yours
that you yourself aren't sure
to call it authentic with its argute features
with all its immortal listlessness.

The sprain mind still anguishes
for subnormal retardness with no reason
without clement of all essence
of nonsensical lenience of serenity
to scamper with the waves of the sound
of cricket's mate with all gusto
of firkin existence of the world
and its universe as well

You grope yourself nowhere
with the allusion of everywhere
although not resilient even for
original essence of life and its mortality
that's the real coaming for the cause of life
and its accomplishment

The nob of liars

She was busy negotiating the price of three gram of DNA est
Everything was ignoring essence seeking the bloody quest

If I say integral and endless feature of your world is betray
Then it wouldn't be a boast but the real reality and its portray

You decorated humanity and all the characteristic of humans
for name sake
To be humanistic human is a curse in your dystopian utopia you make

The nob of liars and their admire
honesty is again curse here with deceived mire

Deceptive inceptions are crystal clear mirror
The very transparency of mind doesn't have error

Cut the cakes of brainy minds
Everything is seduction of all kinds

I surpass myself

A mesmerized smile is an epic with blue
A blink of eyes live an era with all hue

I surpass myself within all in mine
The darkened lit mind will always shine

The existence is nothing but a state of being
Every entry is an exit and a way of leaving

The hidden spikes are there inside the very eyes
Everyone enjoys free-liberty in the holographic skies

Making abstract the concrete is a palace on water
Realities are always before eyes but realized later

The sun is stolen

The hikes of hive with my life
never want nectar with all cliff

The books that create the innovation most
Everything becomes trivial and the essence lost

The belief and faith of lies prosper
The lie's fame is worldwide and hyper

The question isn't of truth at all
But to make lie truth and reality small

I stitch my emotions for every interval of seconds
Crumbling the reckons of mind that dippens

The enlightened lights I feel darkened as well
The sun is stolen and seen on the back of snail

You should skip to wear mask

You should skip to wear mask
because your eyes appeal and ask

The depth of eyes and your smile
activate my pheromones from a mile

All the romantic feelings he deny
Thoughts of heart he feels   annoy

His scattered alienation is his love
Heart always flies in the sky with dove

He finds and creates new ways and path
Even he experiences peace in the wrath

Feelings are feelings and as the emotions
Sigmond and Anna Freud aren't illusions

3.7 shades of grief

A birth is a grief that provides happiness
birth starts the ending
Family is a grief that's loop to seek happiness
though ends in nothing

A grief of death is a dangerous fear of life in life
Grief always brings happiness with it
A death is a grief that ends all the grief
0.7 grief related to mind while dying fit

The connection to the smile of Buddha and Monalisa

The superconscious is Id and unconscious is Ego
to eliminate Superego with worldly folly

I, the nothing of nothing and the quark of being
is a neutron particle to be in no state of being
with the essence of existence and extract of
cosmic consciousness with the connection to
the smile of Buddha and Monalisa

I, the super contradict being wants not to be into being as well

The loans of being is the utmost ghost

The sweet beliefs are the bitter germs
No one show their lose even losing homes

The loans of being is the utmost ghost
Even everyone languishes for it the most

I killed my mind with sharpened nail
Buddha's weapon may be his heads snail

I, the believer never believe in belief
The world is hellish jail, not a relief

The mindly conscience and consciousness of unknowing
The existence blooms natural without seeds and sowing

I let everything go even my very being

The unknown affinity and the known fright
bloom in me with no reason
The reasons that check my existential balance
and I let everything go even my very being

I, the mysterious one is even the same to me
with every known particles of mine

The spiritual kamsutra

A pinkish cotton bud and of that lotus
are the spiritual kamsutra of sky
for the coitus to land
The dying frogs along roadside
defy the meaning of existential essence
with watery smell to determine the fragrance
of all fragrant

The coconut-liquor wants to make me stupor
with Freudian psyche
but the half-opened eyes of Buddha
seem more stupor than anything else

Crow is an abuse

The scattered and innocent-fooled beings
spread themselves around the world
with the strong projection of the wisest wise
The more I dig myself, my mind becomes solid
I want to drink my borewell's water of mind

The thirsty crow has condemned the water
to support Mahad Satyagraha
It's raven that dares to sit on the flying eagle
high in the sky
Crow is an abuse
created and imposed by the arsefuckers
to dominate the real wisest
who are conscious and awaken

I, the scorching petal

Tukoba composes abhang on my nothingness
and creative disinterestedness in the testimony of secular Chhatrapati
whose ballad sung by Mahatma Jotiba

Tukoba meets Babasaheb Ambekar in his press office
Ramai croons Tukoba's abhang with Babasaheb
And Shahu Maharaj smiles at with Bahujan Hitay
The quantum entanglement of my soul is with them all
And resonant with Tukoba

The flow of poetryness in mine percolates
through ideological literariness from Tukoba to Babasaheb
The bouquet of revolution is as fragrant
that the smellers break all thralldom
My writing is the fragrance of the bouquet
and I, the scorching petal
that sprouts the buds

A tilt universe of grain

A tilt universe of grain
can milt the human brain

An aesthetics of political cruelty
still incepted faith in mind of commons
who tend to be wise

The commentary on the contemporariness
starts with very ancient verse
The scientific community
languish for pathetic curse

Grief is real and the happiness is its widow

A boast is reality and reality is virtual
Virtuality determines the truth
Poets hide into the words
while politicians are behind them
Shamelessness is a crucial ornament
and every one is now shame

The names are authentic and truth is shadow
Grief is real and the happiness is its widow
I cannot always think of grief as is always for sure
The importance of its contradict is always more

I show pity on grief because it seems sad

I pluck my leaf with my bloody bud
Though the world is a mire
but I never need its pyre

I disguise a bee to suck my nectar
I play all the roles and I myself is director

I sweeten your poison though your truth is fake
Oceans are enforced to become the lake

The breaths of life sting and I dissipate my perfume
I splurge on my mind though your ideology is vacuum

I play with grief and it dance with me
Its game is high though I am not on knee

I show pity on grief because it seems sad
I feel a little relief to see it enough glad

Eunuch skies reproduce the earthly being

The very sowing of mine
isn't the characteristics of nine

The deception and betrayal I bear
The cocoons of firefly are emotional sheer

The chirping of humanity is deaf
Oceans of my mind still dense and deep

Who keeps what and why this life
I keep myself with sharpened knife

The time that hit my essence of being
Eunuch skies reproduce the earthly being

The hearsay and listen to are your cultural prone

The real educations enhance genuine character
Though all are pimps around and practice barter

Pity is the bravest virtue misunderstood as coward
My mind enlightens and then pyramids are powered

What determine to yourself is your strength
No parameters know my depth and length

The hearsay and listen to are your cultural prone
Your imperial humanity though have humanistic tone

The ass are trivially notorious here as mule and other
May be your essence is more than them and you will never bother

Grief should be called glee with enthusiastic hype

Wives generally skull the man
and however make them null of man

Presumption and reality become the same
Who becomes famous on whose name

The contradiction of life is now usual
Lie is truth and betrayal is casual

The wives and the world are substitute of life
Grief should be called glee with enthusiastic hype

Skipped lives you live with consent and style
Boasts are high but no one walk within a mile

The griefy buds I blossom are exiled by you

The breathes still hurting me
I cannot blame oxygen and even nature
I know my foes, they are still loyal with their enmity
I always spray deaths on me

The smell of fried emotions spread,
I oversee the used palm oil
Grief is sown thrice in a month
and the deceiver is the mother soil

The griefy buds I blossom are exiled by you
The happiness vanish and minds are in queue
I freed my mind and grief gets freed
Happiness even existence not in greed

Your ideology is cruel ethical boast

Your theology and mythological mysteries
are your cultural g-spot
Your ideology is cruel ethical boast
and you pretend your culture as a thought

I spit on your pretence and pompous morality
though you proud on your illegal sovereignty

Your fatherly skies are the bastard colossus spread
Your deities and religion is extortion and based on dread

The prominence you imposed is a coward crown
Your actions words are actually passive noun

You mischievously proclaimed it your Brooklyn

I peel off myself eroding my mind
My layers are rainbow where cruel is kind

The hues of mine are mineless mines
The dozens of skies seem bunches of nines

I enjoy ecstacy from within's shine
Grief's brooks actually flow glee wine

The upside down is downside up
I look myself in my pupil very close up

I lost myself in my kind pity world
Where truth balanced and imagination hold

The sun is cold and poles are none
The life creative and loneliness fun

Everything is reality of all senses feel
An infinite eyed human is real whom you kill

You limit everything and limit yourself
I don't want to be you and never help

The stories you stole are mine routine
You mischievously proclaimed it your Brooklyn

I forgive you all if you find yourself in you
No need to stand in any kind of worldly queue

I rhyme myself into the government scheme

The anima of my body is an animas of my soul
The existence is my psyche and its essence is moul

I live a delusion may be my illusion of life
The life here mirages and of none type

I rhyme myself into the government scheme
Luring for truth here foulness with truth meme

Mythologies, histories are shimmer's truth here
They make manipulation devine and take its care

They replace polity to politicians and make people tool
Blind devotees of them enjoy and smoothing themselves cool

In today's divinity, reading a book is whorish deed

A mental masterbate even intercourse is barren
Social media kicks life and blow high the siren

In today's divinity, reading a book is whorish deed
For living real and satisfying life, what's the need

Childhood is now virtual and adolescence is a game
Cruel exploitations are on going on culture's name

A fearlessness is a sign of frightened mind now
A human being is now paltry and crucial is a cow

It's time to be lonely and be the alone
Cultures are bullshits and civilization is a clone

They lived like mountains

She dried her helplessness
to wet my childhood
He slashed his wildhood
to set my livelihood

Both sacrifice their everything
with theirness to fill me
I am their horizon,
they are ready to merge anywhere to heal me

To show the gratitude and respect for them
is my existential limit
They lived like mountains
and showed life its utmost summit

Hostile of truth is truth of hostile

Hostile of truth is truth of hostile
Nature is taboo for you
and you adore coital carved stones
You manipulate historical Buddhism
to mold your mythological bones

You disgust the ultimate beauties
that used to bloom aesthetic fragrance
You make fake stories to spread as reality
with your bloody false reference

Your generations conceal the truth
and the histories excavate Buddha everywhere
Even the universe is the land of Budhha
You cannot hide everything everywhere
Truth of hostile is hostile of truth …

I have to join the childhood of grief

Relations are the best follies of an honest phoney
and blood relations are the bloody boast crony

Kindness is foul and foul is truth
Truth is lucid dream and unjust is truth

Just and unjust never be sides of the same coin
Humanity is orphan and orphanage is family's shine

I have to join the childhood of grief
What are the life-tales and who can brief

The scream of happiness I assume truth
The rivers flow, though the world is ruth

I inscribe my being on bodhi tree's leaf

Seven point melancholy added in my sorrow
I frequently let go the usual despair arrow

The sadness is a season that blooms in grief
Mind uplift with its innocent mischief

Eudaimonic grief rears existential hedonic
I weave peace within the grief chronic

The life and Budhha are hardware software
A trapped lifer should now become aware

I inscribe my being on bodhi tree's leaf
Let the world be paranoiac and live their sleep

Kind is not kind as usual every time

Sorrowful borrowings you lend me by force
I am not interested to find the grief's main source

The copulation of being is not merely mind
How long life weave itself with golden wind

Kind is not kind as usual every time
Who's unknown that how the word comes lime

The fame of transience is always like its nature
Life is arbitrary but runs by the creature

Lifer always finds an excuse for augustness of life
Though it's not liable so and not of its type

The third world also divided into many

Grief is replaced by anything in life
in the course of time
Nothing changes even the ages and eras
in the course of time

The traditions and rituals you live
are of the biggest blind liar
Political compromises of rights
and helplessness are prior

The third world also divided into many
by the piece of paper that bart
And the cowards assume their sterility art of living
and life's part

Nikola Tesla and the mysteries

Grapes are pyramids of grief
and the grief is wine
The aims and objectives in life
are the same of everyone and of mine

Intoxication not always
deals with wine and sot
It's not always reality
what says your thought

It deals with life which is lived
with all frequencies
The original and pure life is there
with all social and psychological deficiencies

Nikola Tesla and the mysteries
of mine are the same
It's twice and thrice to ask that
who is living on whose name

The patience of mine makes you patient

I wrote poem on publisher's note
My child played it making its boat

The grief of Buddha is happiness for me
My every world is truth and reality for me

The exploitation of mine is my mind
The ecstasy within me is also of my mind

My mind should be mine is my ambition
The world is sick as same is my condition

The patience of mine makes you patient
You assume me your patient is you quotient

The brook waits for me for Nyahari in recess

I work in farm and she is my reaper
The sun is masker and trees are my keeper

The brook waits for me for Nyahari in recess
Shadow loves to take my life into its process

The dews of sweat wipe the entire day
The soil is divine giver and art is its clay

The sky is prompter though mountains never speak
How long shall I stand on my dead body's heap?

The gratitude towards Babasaheb I bow to live
No one is getting here the real freedom's clue

The sympathy is dice and they win our pace

The rights of poor are business for rich
Their kindness is noble like the bloody leech

The pity and compassion are their fashionable business
The sympathy is dice and they win our pace

The rumors they spread becomes our reality
We stick with the principles with fake reality

They operate social media to divert us from truth
We enjoy public toilets as open voting booth

They act fool to show that we are wise to make fool
We react genuine and accept litter as precious wool

But actually they are mule

Untouchability is an abuse by Hindus
to Hindus themselves
They hide their inability by this
and plenty afraid the blues

The conspiracy and assassination
they do with guile
They proclaim themselves thoroughbred
but actually they are mule

Their impotence and sterility
blooms with time
Their being is as fake
as they plagiarized hymn

Their ownership they self-proclaim divine
It's trivial than the bloody nugatory wine

Ferocity is on peak

Your foolish childlike act
you inculcate innocent
You're dark within and out
with darkened fluorescent

You are divine cruel
with cultural cyanide
You are social leech
and existential termite

You're stigma on humanity
since you deceive your soul
Ferocity is on peak
you are bloody moal

This is the an abhorrent life

Nothing happens in my life
as per my wish
The entwine of my dreams
I always cherish

My expectations and my essence
are though contradict
But it's the requirement of existence
to live the unpredict

This is the an abhorrent life
I don't want to accept it
Though it seems excuse but
I have responsibilities
and I have to respect it

The earthworms become my intestines

I can see the fatherly affection
in the eyes of working bull in the field
The entire life of humans
is nothing but the readymade yield

The earthworms become my intestines
and butterflies the tongue
I eat the entire sky
and oceans become the young

The wipers bite my being
and existence become life
The dead flexibility is immortal
and mortal death alife

Though my virgin ideology is tool of your cure

I offer my celibacy to the nature
and nature become virgin woman
I untie my belly button
and you still call it cumin

The pure sand of ocean becomes pure
everytime with every tide
My life is bloody sot and cruelly whip me
with every ride

The pure oceans, rivers are in the world
and the entire world is impure
My childish philosophy is like your life
Though my virgin ideology is tool of your cure

Once upon a time I was my own being

Once upon a time I was my own being
I have distributed myself to an attached ones
and they assumed me china goods
Now I feel nothing and regret with pity
wishing if I were the dark and deep woods

Once upon a time I was my own being
The existence I attire is a world house of mine
I already freed my being, freeing my conscious
The unconscious forest now lightened with Buddha
I left myself and even cast away from subconscious

Once upon a time I was my own being
The permanence of energy is energy itself
There is nothing permanent even quantum possibilities
The worlders made the entire world even mental state
The pure pimp market with all the commodities

I still believe in judiciary, not in who run it by law

I was finding innocently precious dry gems in the mud
All it was all seem delicious food but actually was stale curd

I graze my mind in the pasture of imagination and its beyond
The heart I freed is always feel to live in the remand

Deceptive facts and realities of law is manipulation of judiciary
Corrupt police are now the pillars of justice and its machinery

Knowing the truth, judges expect commons to believe in them
Even they will agree that they themselves are the bloody shame

I still believe in judiciary, not in who run it by law
Being a common, once I will scratch it by my lion paw

I am at fault

She kills my desires to live with satisfaction
Moronly she is wise and justify every action

I won't call her river as she limits the freedom
An innocent essence she always finds boredom

I am at fault to break the shackles of her slavery
Even she wasn't aware of it and was living it as bravery

Sometimes virtue of help and kindness seem futile to me
Cage birds now afraid to sky and they peck for flee

Their darkness is their reality while the light is a taboo
They adore their slavery giver and appreciate all its coo

It's not 'she' only who is living this trap, there is 'he' and 'it' also
They feel the trap an ocean but it's not even a common corso

I am the great sugar pine

I need to evolve my tongue to speak the lie
The world is true for liars' sky

Honesty is outdated, humanity is expired
Instead briskness for deceit is hired

The values, morals and ethics (not of imperial) are soft timber
Today's smartness is termite that gets out of number

But I feel evolution is so slow so mutation is fine
Though you assume yourself highest monument,
I am the great sugar pine

I, the dust of being is a disease of life

I have to empty my heart today itself
How many poems or any other literary device
come to help me to alleviate
I want to vomit the entire existentiality now
The spur of life is not existential now
I, the dust of being is a disease of life
The desert is groom and the living is its hype

What I feel that I deal

What I feel that I deal
you be the pimp the whore I will nil

The worldly ways I condemn with zeal
I know whom I have to kill

You will exile me but not my thought
I never count business mindly   what I got

I hit the fork even my former ideology
I just live as I want with all my cozy

The life, the world, the grief I piss off
My dear world ! with lovely hate I be off